CAPITALIST-SOCIALIST PARTY OF AMERICA

CapSoc

CSPA

outskirts press

Doctrines and Adherence and Outline

Many communists are waking up not understanding why the sudden decline in their government and system whereby they are being governed. The decline of absolute communism was inevitable. The outstanding reasons as any businessman or businesswoman worth their salt could see were by no means insidious in developing and that communism was dooming itself and from inception it had been flawed.

Marxism and Leninism espoused theories on government that were based solely on self-supporting systems, or, one that was more one-sided than pragmatic. In other words, they felt that their theories and ideology, as well as philosophy were absolutely sound to thwart off any other system of governing and to surpass it economically and politically in its five-year programs. However, both men failed to realize a simple flaw in their theories on communism and its five-year programs. As Napoleon and Hitler both had realized a simple error in trying to conquer the Siberian Arctic freeze and not preparing their troops properly in clothes to withstand the elements of the Arctic cold, they succumbed in the end to their failures to do so. Both Marx and Lenin likewise failed to realize that communism in theory and pragmatism was competing against no one but itself and not the outside economic world and stock markets around the world that controlled the bartering of world oil, gas, gold, platinum, silver, grain foods and natural resources of countries, as well as imports and exports commodities of countries. By not adhering to a capitalist regiment of any kind and ways of doing things in an open world market that was orientated from its inception in a capitalist mode of world trade and daily transactions, communism and its five-year programs had no one to compete against but itself. World trade is capitalistic in makeup and not socialistic. Remember, you sell to the highest and lowest bidders, not as one of absolute communism that does not know the value of a world market and that of free trade, whereas, under communism the state dictates what is sold and not sold and how it is sold and for how much. Communism had no other major political parties to compete against in Russia. We all know that no country is self-sufficient in all natural resources and must trade with other countries to get those things it needs for its vital existence. Communism has no means of competing with world trade because of the very esoteric structure of it economic system that relies on socialist programs and ideology. Five-years programs for crops and factories production were sometime favorable, but viable ways of dealing with world trade centers were not there because the designers of communism forgot about the two most important things there are in transacting business, the entrepreneur, and the ownership of private property, whereby, the state gave the people the right of ownership of property and merchandise, as well as the right to have their own businesses as long as they do not interfere with state functions. Communism puts the major industries and businesses in the hands of government control and not that of private enterprise. Thus, commodities produced in five-year communist programs would have to go through the world market to be sold and avoid being underbidded by other countries. However, the communists were not gifted as capitalists in gaining buyers for their products. In short, the world stock markets are capitalist in makeup and exploitations. Communism does not believe in capitalist ideology and ways of doing things. Thus, five-year programs would fail for the simple reasons traders at home could not get what they wanted on paper for their programs, and a time limit placed on programs would not allow such five-year programs to always work out because of the capitalist orientated world free trade market and its ups and downs. Many Russian government workers and private citizens could not get paid for their work because of this, slowly dividing the country.

From the beginning of world trade and barter, mankind has always traded and bartered in gold or other comparable commodities and precious stones. In short, money or precious stones that represented it are our chief means of world trade and has been from the inception of men trading with one another. Socialism does not believe in capitalism or bothers with how it works, but their own constitutions and laws that espouse a communist politburo or one of socialism in makeup omitting capitalist free trade and the understanding of how money works as we see today in Russian satellite countries trying to understand the capitalist system and world trade markets. Any government, be it capitalist or socialist, must have a budget and must have daily business transactions. In short, a government dealing in world trade must understand the basic principles of capitalism and what is right and wrong for it. In short, a government is a business. How could Marx and Lenin both overlooked this simple aspect that any mediocre private entrepreneur would tell you is the epitome of doing business in bartering and trading. On paper, communism is a beautiful system, or so it seems. But in actuality, it would be almost impossible for communism to survive without some form of capitalism and capitalistic knowledge of its functioning in the competitive capitalist world of free trade. In pragmatism, absolute communism does not work, only on paper.

At the same time many cannot see the failures of capitalism around the world as a viable means of fighting off world economic decay. Whereas, capitalist countries are slowly digging their graves due to rising inflation, unemployment, recessionary periods and depressionary ones that are getting longer, and a sedentary lifestyle that leads to obesity and many other health problems. Under the capitalist system as outlined, a handful of people, usually less than ten-percent of the populace, control the wealth and stock markets of a country. This is not only true in America but capitalist countries throughout the world, whereby a handful of people decide the economic stability of that country's wealth and well being. The masses often beg for food, clothes and medical treatment of some satisfaction, as well as jobs and housing. The failure of the absolute capitalist system envisioned by its forefathers and many, coincides with absolute communism failure as being a viable system in the long run and is inevitably doomed for failure. It would destroy itself because capitalism believes in the greatest profit (at any cost, be it war, stealing, mendacity and deception, slavery, caste system, colonialism, etc) for the lowest wages being paid out to laborers. By out competing bidders, one reaps the cream of the crop. Marx said that artisans prostitute their skills and labor out to the greatest bidders of pay for them. Marx wanted to do away with the bourgeoisie, which is needed for trading. In the United States we see jobs by the millions being lost to foreign countries in Asia, Africa, South America and countries that have no minimum wage laws whereby workers can earn a profitable pay from their labor. World trade and labor forces see capitalism slowly destroying western country after country from the lost of jobs and technology of capital countries to other countries that can provide the cheapest labor for the highest of profits for businesses and corporations. This cycle of capitalist countries losing jobs and wealth at home for its workers, and slowly becoming desperate for finances for themselves, will not go away, but persist as you are seeing today.

It should be obvious to any high school student that the United States had to change much of its rhetoric and programs concerning capitalism making them more applicable and viable to those of socialism, believe it or not. In example, Franklin Roosevelt and his New Deal had to adopt many socialist programs and even socialist ideology as far as governing, in order to save the United States during the Great Depression that started in 1929, or so they say. Without implementing programs like the WWW, WPA, public housing laws for the poor, as well as public welfare, social security laws, government intervention into how banks are regulated; transportation laws for the highways, as well as government intervention into military life and its integration, the United States would be much different today as a nation. Even the names of many of these programs that still exist from the Rooseveltian era, utilizes the word social, connotating socialism in its meaning and early forms. Rich people do not as a rule spend their wealth on public programs for masses because even though they are rich, they still can not come up with yearly income for such programs, whereby, the government collects it through taxation from its populace. In the last fifty years or so in the United States, we have seen big government hands into how things are being ran at home. Government bureaucracy, likewise, is getting out of hand here in America. There is simply too much red tape in doing business with the United States government.

At the same time, many cannot see the failure of the capitalist system around the world in its absolutionism, slowly coming apart.

Whereby, capitalist countries of Europe and the Americas are slowly coming apart, and the inflation of goods, unemployment, recessions and depressions are as real as the people that experience them. Even in America the richest country in the world economically, we see many going hungry and several thousand cases of people dying of starvation are reported yearly, but not publicized my the media for fear of how it would make American propaganda look abroad and to the rest of the world. Here's a country that gives away billions each year in food and foreign aid, but will not feed its own citizens, but let them layup and starve to death. First lady, Mrs. Bush, goes on national television in ads asking the American people to help feed and clothes its poor, unbelievable, but true.

By combining socialism (government control of major industries, transportation, utilities, banks and other businesses that control a high percentage of the GNP) and capitalism, we come at a realization of what CapSoc (Capitalist-Socialist Party Of America) is all about. Here, a rotation of power to city-states types of governments must be realized to ensure its success. This in no way violates any country's laws that are based on democratic vote and freedom of expression. Abuse of CapSoc is not permitted or the degradation of any country or people. CapSoc adds to the dignity of mankind and people that believe in an equality of life, and a government free from tyranny, despots, and any kind of totalitarian state. In short, any country is as good as its laws that govern it and those that carry out those laws are its safeguard against any internal or external forces that would abuse them.

CapSoc uses the highest forms of leadership based on morality that governs us. CapSoc does not adhere to past records of it followers, but a pledged-vow of allegiance. Those that govern us have made mistakes like those it rule over, an understanding of what is right and wrong is needed to safeguard those rights and liberties as put forth and advocated by CapSoc. Our leadership is never based on Machiavellian philosophy, but sound morality as put forth by those who believe in ethics and a fair government for the people. CapSoc sets out its laws, principles of morality for its public officials. (*1 CapSocs Manual of Ethics) Our rank is not broken by any and any hanky-panky like tampering with votes, human and legal rights, property, and wealth is not out objectives. CapSoc never tolerates stealing and killing, discrimination, maltreatment of people. CapSoc does believe in resistance when subversive people arise to meet that need, however. Those that have the gaining of personal wealth and personal power are not true CapSocs. In America, we have only a two-party system, whereby, the Democrats and Republicans play political football with our lives. Here we find much deceit, mendacity by government, stealing and many other crimes by government to it citizens, and many unaware of what is going on at city, state and federal levels of government. The United States is being stolen blind at all levels of government. This is being publicized more and will continue to be alarming to many citizens. CapSoc will be the third-political party in America giving the people another choice of governing themselves.

CapSoc has a judicial, legislative and executive make-up. The congress will only supercede city and state when it feels laws or political actions are warranted to insure equal and impartial justice and administration. CapSoc puts less emphasis on the executive and federal levels; the city-state orientational approach is desired with the executive and other branches of government looking in on them. Then, under CapSoc, your government officials at the lower levels of government are as well trained and knowledgeable of government as those at the top of government. When fighting a cancerous tumor, one goes to the source of that tumor to eradicate it at whatever means. By controlling the growth of this tumor, one thwarts its growth, being able to destroy it. You don't put your best technicians and doctors in the operating room at the last moment, but to use them early and not to lead to a more serious problem. Broader power is given to mayors, councilmen, aldermen, city and county agencies. Why? To stop any situation from getting worst, you go to it at the most earliest of opportunities. This rotation of power from the upper levels of government to lower government officials must have the best workers to carry out social programs. Upper levels of government will continue to advise and offer ideas and programs, but it is at the grassroots of government that these programs are implemented as we see much failure in the federal government today in America in carrying out many of its social programs due to mismanagement of funds, stealing of money and merchandise, discrimination, etc. CapSoc is not giving its power entirely to the city-states and doing away with the other levels of governmental powers, but the emphasis of power is being rotated more to the city-states where many of the problems originate in governing the masses. The executive and federal branch of government, as well as congress (legislature) will still have the highest powers of authority, only paying more attention to the city-states that has gained power in implementing programs. Hence, the federal government and bureaucracy will set up offices and headquarters in city-state communities to overseer and gain more knowledge of what is going on throughout the city-state communities. Likewise, would the governors of city-states have power over the city-states governments, but would act as a perfunctionary of overseeing executive level policies being carried out as implemented through the city-state programs. Their powers would be in outlining these programs with the city-state executive branch of government. A state budget would be no more than the cost of running the city-state government as outlined by the higher branches of government that has the final say. Legislature representation of the state would meet the same fate, no more than a safeguard of the city-state system of that state. Power is being giver to the city-state government through the upper branches of government. It is the people who make a government; therefore, the power must start with them in a democratic society. Government workers only carry out the peoples wishes of how they are to be governed under CapSoc. The people make public servants.

All laws must be given the final vote of approval by the federal and executive and legislative branches and not states. The city and state must adhere to these laws. We can see all around us the chaos of each states laws and how they cause us so much trouble and money being spent on them in implementation of these laws. Discrimination in any law makes them unsound, if not unjust to those under it. *CapSoc Party believes in unity of state laws and their conformity. For each state to have their own judicial laws would make room for a lot of headaches at the upper echelons of government as we see all around us the burden that the federal government is carrying to overseer state laws and regulation, often the federal government must implement its owns laws to overseer how states are being ran. We see this in businesses like airplanes, trains, highways laws and money to build them; ships at sea, housing, schools, hospital programs such as Medicaid, Medicare; hence, the federal and executive branch of government in America must overseer much of what the state does in many of its programs as mentioned. To deny a person the rights given another because of locale is unjust. This is absurd when one weighs this with the impartiality of justice that the federal government is to adhere to. How can a government be impartial when each state has its own laws that it goes by? It is the duty of national government to have a check and balance on laws and rights of the individual within each state and city. Our legal system is very chaotic and biased in performance to the blindness of justice one is to receive; and this becomes more apparent on the appeal of laws at the state and federal level, showing the ineptness of the system.[1] Thus, have the United States government and United States Supreme Court implementing for e.g., civil rights laws that are impartial to all states, as well as commerce laws, criminal laws, etc.

CapSoc is unique in that it places the power in the hands of those that need it and would best implement laws of the land and would likewise have a first hand knowledge of how things are being ran. Under CapSoc, the private ownership of property and merchandise that one works for would still exist. Innately, human beings desire ownership of some kind of property or merchandise and will do almost anything to obtain this personal ownership of commodities. Private ownership of property and merchandise is also a necessity for its survival in the world free trade and marketing. It is the epitome of free trade and what people around the world work for: something to call their own, and at the same time keep that identity of individuality. Working for something to call your own is inspiring and enhances the will of the creative person and does not hinder freedom of expression.

Under CapSoc the vital industries to a country (transportation, utilities, major industries and corporations, medical programs, etc) are placed in the hands of the government to ensure that the people will get the best for their tax money and not being monopolized by private ownership disrupting normal usage of these vital industries. We have seen in capitalistic countries where private ownership of public utilities has caused excessive and unfair rates. Government intervention is always needed to offset the greed of many capitalist pigs that monopolize all at any price or consequences for the masses. Strikes that can cripple corporation and nations must be offset by government intervention, especially when they are of vital needs like energy, transportation, utilities, housing, etc. Mankind has not learned to know when to stop greed, avarice of capital for a handful and not benefiting the masses. People are at a mercy to wealth and power and must be legislated into putting the essentials of life and others first and not themselves. History has shown us that society and a country will fail in the end when this is not checked.

In countries like England, France, Italy, United States and Germany, we see socialist parties and forms of it in governing the people going on. These socialist parties work along side capitalist ones in establishing fair play for it citizens. These countries would be in economic decay if not for socialist programs being adopted by the masses to keep them going and compensate for the inadequacies of the capitalist national budgets that fail to solve the social problems of a nation. This is not a misnomer, as socialist parties and programs have grown tremendously in recent years throughout Europe and the world. Many people around the world are realizing that large private industry will not take care of the masses in the long run, but put money into rich peoples' coffers. It is the people who must support their own efforts to proper representation of people to public offices to carry out their programs and social efforts. Both socialism and capitalism are here to stay, but there must be symmetry of both; although in the long run socialism will predominate as the favorite government to adhere to and live under simply because of its pragmatism.

Socialism came before capitalism anthropologists tell us because the small world population had little need for want of food and clothes. It was only when population changed and avarice that earlier rulers did little to satisfy the masses with the same wealth they had amassed. Capitalism is more of a one-on-one, whereby, socialism represents the control of a larger body of people. However, both systems go way back in time, although called otherwise. To use both capitalism and socialism would form the most powerful government the world has ever seen. If the world was once destroyed by water, (flood) people will succumb to one based only on capitalism or socialism alone. In short, if people cannot see the viableness of a system and way of life, they will simply not accept it, but fall with their fallibilities. It is up to the people and no one else to decide their future as to what type of government they will live under. Capitalism is an intrinsic way of life, as is social programs for the masses altruistically and osmotically with us. This is CapSoc in essence, the realization of both capitalism and socialism within a nation. CapSoc believe as well in the American dream of self-expression and the freedom of a people, no matter how different that belief may be. We defend those rights of all men to aspire to their personal goals.

In the treatment of many diseases one drug or therapy is in itself not a cure or alleviation of that ailment, but a combination of drugs and more than one type of therapy is needed. Most serums for cures of our ailments will not stand alone if only one drug or component is used, but a combination of other drugs and their components do we perfect a cure and a remedy to what ails us. Isn't it about time we applied some of this same logic, reasoning, to our chaotic political systems and governments around the world?

In the last 200 years we have seen governments doing little to cut down on pollution of air, water and land based factories. We find this very true in capitalist countries as well as some socialist countries that place a higher value on their budgets and five-year work programs. Both systems blame one another for the pollution of the earth. It is obvious that both are at fault due to the oversight and failures by both to set down proper guidelines against pollution and the destroying of green plant life. Our ecological environment must be safeguarded if we are to live here on planet earth, as few environment scientists would tell you otherwise. We must ask ourselves can we continue to live this way? Or, is there other alternative to resolving us from digging our own graves?

CapSoc emphasizes health and ecology first. Would you burn down your house to live outside in the elements of nature? Non-pollution of environment would not harm economic and social programs of a country but would only help in the long run ensure such programs. Countries would still want to trade in commodities. Look at the billions of dollars the United States, China and Russia loses each year to pollution. This same lost money could easily be used to correct many social programs such as housing, job creations, medical treatments and even income for it citizens.

CapSoc emphasizes simplicity. The less bureaucracy we see in government and red tape, the more efficiently that body of government can operate. Mankind has not learned to simplify the things that need simplication, but only complicating them. Intelligent and educated people are coming to realize that the more advance one comes in technology the need for simplicity is most needed. Most people in their college majors, and even if they majored in more than one subject, there are hundreds and thousands of other subjects they are limited in knowledge. Did I call money here? We have created a host of complexities from problems that should not be complex. A conundrum of problems exists in our governments absorbing our governments in a chaotic maze of misery, not only for it citizenry, but those inside government as well. Such a chaotic government breeds waste, greed, poor management and defeat for itself in the end. Just as you check your car for flaws, a government should have a check-and-balance system to overseer its proper maintenance. CapSoc does this in its check-and-balancing at all levels of government.

New cabinets under CapSoc are rare since what we call a circle or cycle that revolves to protect itself. The creation of new laws and cabinets only tell one that the system of government is not working. Hence, the same problems are still there, thus, why is a new cabinet or new laws needed to solve those same old problems? Records only represent what you want them to represent.

Owenites in England, Debites and Larouchites in America, Marxists in Russia and many other political parties were created to put forth socialist programs and agendas to solve social ills. None of these political parties thought to combine both systems, coexisting as one and not trying to do away with the other. Utopia is always beautiful on paper.

Socialism is real as is the science and political system of socialism.

The ownership of private property must bring a tax on such property, but at the same time not being excessive. A personal tax on income is not desired under CapSoc. Why? The collection of personal and business and property taxes go back thousand of years. As in ancient times and even medieval times of serf, lords and peons, we saw a disparage in unfairness in such systems, whereby, kings, pharaohs, governors became rich, as masses ate slop and lived likewise. It is always the duty of government to collect taxes. There are many ways government can collect taxes outside the ways they collect them today and in olden days. Kings that did not like adversaries becoming too rich and building armies against them levied enormous taxes against them. Some of the kings human rights foes were imprisoned, killed and even ostracized from the land they had called their own. Under CapSoc there would be no need for such since laws are there to offset such people from building armies and fortunes that take away from the masses and social programs that would do likewise. A person can still have a fortune, being a millionaire or even billionaire, only that his or her wealth does not interfere with the masses and vital programs that are needed by the people of a country. In short, the government by it laws sees that the vital programs of a nation are safeguarded and any private wealth takes away nothing from the people and social programs of a country. Under CapSoc the emphasis of a government is to take its taxes right off the top, all money has a tax on it. How can this be so? Business that employed are taxed and not the personal income of a person. Hence, taxes are taken out of business payrolls. There are no tax loopholes as under capitalist systems. Everyone and every business are subjected to taxation in one way or the other. Corporate, private, etc owned businesses are all taxed. Under CapSoc the church must likewise give to Cesar what is his in the form of taxes. The church is a business and has its own government as put forth in its creeds, doctrines and laws. We see in many countries, churches getting government grants and money, but paying no tax money, only taking away from the masses and poor and becoming richer. The church has no conscious when it comes to collecting money from the government, but it will not pay taxes. Then, why interfere in government programs when you do not want to become a part of it? This is being very hypocritical wouldn't you say?

There then, must be a separation of state from all religion, including the catering of churches wanting government money. Alternatively, the church will carry its load as others are doing in paying taxes if it is to receive government money. CapSoc honors the free will of man to worship his or her god. In short, CapSoc is not opposing the freedom of religion, but condoning its freedom of that expression, as long as it does not function within the government in getting it to adhere to its beliefs. This includes religion parties being viable as governing the people, but not the mixing of that religion or church with politics. In short, until the church governs the masses, then, the state has control over how it is being run and how far the church can influence it.

Remember, the government is a business and under CapSoc, you, the people, have created this business to help run your daily lives because you cannot work for food and livelihood and try and run the country at the same time. Therefore, you elected to political officials, those you feel can best help you run your daily lives. In addition, in the United States we see billions of dollars being never collected by the government tax agency, as well as many big corporations paying no taxes at all, and of course, the church we just mentioned. In short, the United States government could save billions each year in trying to collect lost taxes and imprisoning people, by adhering to a new way of collecting taxes.

The government of CapSoc is not only concerned about its workers, but all aspect of human life that concerns the welfare of its people. The collection of garbage should be just as important as organizing a union or club to benefit workers. Every aspect of life must we be concerned with and what affect every citizen.

History has proven mankind motives in the usurping of power of government due to economic and political decay. When the moral decadence of any society is apparent, people have resorted to arming themselves to bring about changes. The bullet or the ballot, people have said, and whichever they felt the more apropos. This is only human nature and sense of survival to live a better life free of tyranny, chaos, moral and economic decay. The masses know when things can be better for them and will act according to bring about that change. At no time does CapSoc advocate violence or armament of others to do so. This comes as only an occurrence of human nature to various situation that call for such, but not being advocate by us, only that all democratic processes are in order. As stated earlier, the people of a country historically have decided this fate and how they should be governed and by what means.

A class-conscious society will still exist under CapSoc. There will always be people who want to remain poor for whatever reasons. People wanting wealth will always be with us and there are many that only want to live modestly. Human nature is this way and why tamper with it. No government can force a person to be wealthy or force wealth upon that individual who doesn't want it. Neither can a country force education or morality upon it people, but only getting them to live within the laws. These things, as many nations are learning, are voluntary, although looking very good on paper when you can say a country is 100% literate, or has a 100% believers in a god. Not even all the angels in heaven believed in their creator. The enactment of laws to prevent poverty, illiteracy and non-belief in that deity, cannot change something as innate as human nature and thought and what that individual desires. It is the governing bodies of a country duty to control these people behavior and lifestyle that is most favorable to the state, not hampering in any way that lifestyle. Here we have the epitome of government function; no one faction is offended by the other, but works in unison as a whole rather than a faction. This is very difficult, as history has shown us.

A government must be able to feed its people, provide work for them, housing, medical treatment, as well as controlling those vital industries, corporations, transportation, utilities, etc. Above all, government must inspire its citizens to want to do these things and take the necessary action to do so. Where there is no concern for governmental functions, there is no concern for self. A government is always its people and their concerns.

Even a prostitute that sells her body, (commodity) in turns desire ownership of that body. Under capitalism, the prostitute sells her merchandise (body) to the highest of bidders. The socialist buyer of the prostitute likewise wants ownership of that body, even if for a short time. Here we have a paradox, non-utopian of both capitalism and socialism coexisting. It is only human nature in wanting to own something, even if ones body. It is also human nature in wanting to share things with others and to co-exist. Hence, here we find socialism and the government control of major industries and resources to allow all access to them. Capitalism will always coexist in some form even under a socialist regime. Likewise will socialism always be needed to keep a check-and-balance between the rich and poor; not having one hogging all the wealth, and the controlling of vital resources, industries and utilities.

Both World War I and II are considered economic wars whereby the countries that perpetuated them were countries lacking in natural resources such as gas, oil, minerals and things it could not obtain at home but had to get from elsewhere. From ancient times, history is redundant in the collapse of countries from inflation, recessions and depressions.

The largest world body of peace is the United Nations. It has many agencies including that of world labor and employment, as well as that of world trade. Until world countries agree to establish workable guidelines whereby all countries can satisfactory trade with others, the world will see others wars as World War I and II taking place and over those same things for countries existence. Then, if not the United Nations to help solve problems, we still need some world control on tariffs and international trading of resources and very soon. Even natural water is becoming depleted around the world and this problem must be looked at closely and soon. (*2 The California Water Plan) A handful of nations should never be able to dictate the trade in natural resources and imports to countries, but all nations should be able to decide. Mr. Santyana comes to mind and to paraphrase him: "Those that do not heed the past, will repeat it."

If we are to live here on earth, then, a number must likewise be placed on world population and who we can feed and take care of. Children are born every day to starve to death and die from no medical treatment. In short, we have no way of taking care of them or showing them the love and understanding they should have from parents. Too many of these children are homeless, in poverty, illiterate and diseased. No god meant children to live this way and the degrading and devaluing of human life as we now see it around the world.

The economy of a country influences its morality and even religious beliefs. A person who is starving will steal, kill, lie and even perform lewd sexual acts so that he or she might have food to eat or money in their pockets. This is not contrary to human nature that seeks out self-preservation and some means of livelihood in keeping sanity and equilibrium in daily life.

We have a duality in our lives and just as evil and good are two good examples of it, capitalism and socialism are two others. Sooner or later capitalism and socialism must realize that they must depend on another, each to the best advantage of the other. This duality is a bond, not a division between the two, but stands as a reinforcement of the other in working in harmony for that nation.

Any world government of the future must rely on some forms of socialism to be a viable system. Likewise, capitalism will always exist in some form or another, as there are those who want wealth and those who do not. Human nature and motives will always vary.

Let Us Stand As One

(A song of CapSoc)

Let us stand as one,
One people under the sun.
Our strength is in our unity,
Mankind we love and not disunity.
Those that hunger and thirst, let them be fed;
Those in bondage, freedom shall they be led.
Let us stand as one,
One people under the sun.
CapSoc is for all;
And so shall we call.
Let the people around the world hear our voice.
That they might make a choice,
Between what is right and wrong,
In freedom we grows strong.
Let us stand as one,
One people under the sun.
Working people around the world unite,
In our struggles for peace that we ignite.
Our forefathers lay down the groundwork,
Let us continue their work.
Let us stand as one,
Our work to be done.

End

Epilogue

One of the most powerful countries in the world has trouble feeding many of its people, as well as clothing and housing them. A decline in jobs and personal check payments have declined. Former President Gorborchev wanting to correct many of the flaws and short comings of communism in Russia, could only concede in the end that communism was not the ultimate governing system for the Russian people, but would need some forms of capitalism and western entrepreneurship to help it out.

Countries in Eastern Europe started to distant themselves from her control with the Russian government, because of internal economic ails, being able to do little about it. The worlds trade is based on capitalism in the exchange and the selling of goods, whereby, communism preaches just the opposite; Gorborchev and eastern satellites of Russia realizing the inadequacies of communism (state run and controlled) in competing with capitalist countries around the world. Although Marx and Lenin could produce large momentary economic gains for their system of governing, they would be doomed in the end and long run by the failure of the communist system in competing with capitalist theorists who controlled the world economic marketing trade. Even the Russian space program is suffering from lack of funding.

Communism is its biggest enemy in a capitalist orientated free world marketing of goods and finances. It stunts its own growth as Marx and Lenin would soon find out because it has no one but itself to compete against in the marketing and production of goods and not being self-sufficient in natural resources and other commodities. Where parallel competition is needed as a motivator of human competition, it is lacking here. It feeds on itself and not the world market of competition that controls its existence in a capitalist world of free trade; hence, the word Free Trade! Socialism is based on state and non-private ownership; Capitalism offers private ownership and freedom of trade. In brevity, socialism is not designed to compete in a free world market. This was the biggest mistake that Marx and Lenin never realized. In retrospect, it makes one think that neither Marx nor Lenin really understood the world of marketing and the nature of men and women. Marx and Lenin, people only prostitute their bodies and skills because they choose to do so. Their mistake is being felt throughout the world as the U.S.S.R, (now dissolved into several countries) along with other former communist countries are changing their ways of life, adopting more the theories of capitalism and its capabilities; as is capitalism turning more toward socialism in order to survive here in America. Marx and Lenin saw communism in a utopian sense. Utopians of any kind, overlooks one of the most important things, that of human variables, as well as those non-human. Absolute communism was no more than utopian dreams, being unpragmatic in a capitalist world trade market. Marx and Lenin theories were doomed to failure by its very nature and adherence to absolutionism.

At the same time, many cannot see the failure of the capitalist system around the world in its absolutionism slowly coming apart. Whereby, capitalist countries of Europe and the Americas are slowly coming apart and the inflation of goods, unemployment, recessions and depressions are as real as the people that experience them are.

The CapSoc Party of America at no time tries to make everyone equal. We are only equal in creation. CapSoc though gives everyone an equal opportunity to aspire to their goals of endeavors whatever they may be. To say that all men and women are of the same abilities and desires in life would be deceiving ourselves. Freedom of choice under a democratic functioning is the goal of CapSoc and not to try and make all people equal in abilities, but equality in choice of destiny and goals that are aspired to.

*1 CapSoc Manual of Ethics is given to workers of the CapSoc Party.

*2 The California Water Plan is a confidential plan to utilize sea water (Pacific Ocean) to help solve the shortage of water in California and other western states, especially those states that use the Colorado River. It is drawn up by scientists of the CapSoc Party (?)

Information on Individual States References of Officials, Addresses, Telephone Numbers and Other Data Concerning Capsoc Parties

THIS SECTION ALSO INCLUDES TERRITORIES OF THE UNITED STATES.

CAPSOC PARTY OF ALABAMA (AL)
DIRECTOR
ADDRESS
PHONE NO.
INCEPTION
LEGAL STAFF
MEMBERSHIP
MAJOR PROGRAMS COMPLETED
MISC.

CAPSOC PARTY OF ALASKA (AK)
DIRECTOR
ADDRESS
PHONE NO.
INCEPTION
LEGAL STAFF
MEMBERSHIP
MAJOR PROGRAMS COMPLETED
MISC.

CAPSOC PARTY OF ARKANSAS (AR)
DIRECTOR
ADDRESS
PHONE NO.
INCEPTION
LEGAL STAFF
MEMBERSHIP
MAJOR PROGRAMS COMPLETED
MISC.

CAPSOC PARTY OF ARIZONA (AZ)
DIRECTOR
ADDRESS
PHONE NO.
INCEPTION
LEGAL STAFF
MEMBERSHIP
MAJOR PROGRAMS COMPLETED
MISC.

CAPSOC PARTY OF CALIFORNIA (CA)
DIRECTOR
ADDRESS
PHONE NO.
INCEPTION
LEGAL STAFF
MEMBERSHIP
MAJOR PROGRAMS COMPLETED
MISC.

CAPSOC PARTY OF COLORADO (CO)
DIRECTOR
ADDRESS
PHONE NO.
INCEPTION
LEGAL STAFF
MEMBERSHIP
MAJOR PROGRAMS COMPLETED
MISC.

CAPSOC PARTY OF CONNECTICUT (CT)
DIRECTOR
ADDRESS
PHONE NO.
INCEPTION
LEGAL STAFF
MEMBERSHIP
MAJOR PROGRAMS COMPLETED
MISC.

CAPSOC PARTY OF DELAWARE (DE)
DIRECTOR
ADDRESS
PHONE NO.
INCEPTION
LEGAL STAFF
MEMBERSHIP
MAJOR PROGRAMS COMPLETED
MISC.

CAPSOC PARTY OF DISTRICT OF COLUMBIA (DC)
DIRECTOR
ADDRESS
PHONE NO.
INCEPTION
LEGAL STAFF
MEMBERSHIP
MAJOR PROGRAMS COMPLETED
MISC.

CAPSOC PARTY OF FLORIDA (FL)
DIRECTOR
ADDRESS
PHONE NO.
INCEPTION
LEGAL STAFF
MEMBERSHIP
MAJOR PROGRAMS COMPLETED
MISC.

CAPSOC PARTY OF GEORGIA (GA)
DIRECTOR
ADDRESS
PHONE NO.
INCEPTION
LEGAL STAFF
MEMBERSHIP
MAJOR PROGRAMS COMPLETED
MISC.

CAPSOC PARTY OF HAWAII (HI)
DIRECTOR
ADDRESS
PHONE NO.
INCEPTION
LEGAL STAFF
MEMBERSHIP
MAJOR PROGRAMS COMPLETED
MISC.

CAPSOC PARTY OF IDAHO (ID)
DIRECTOR
ADDRESS
PHONE NUMBER
INCEPTION
LEGAL STAFF
MEMBERSHIP
MAJOR PROGRAMS COMPLETED
MISC.

CAPSOC PARTY OF ILLINOIS (IL)
DIRECTOR
ADDRESS
PHONE NO.
INCEPTION
LEGAL STAFF
MEMBERSHIP
MAJOR PROGRAMS COMPLETED
MISC.

CAPSOC PARTY OF INDIANA (IN)
DIRECTOR
ADDRESS
PHONE NO.
INCEPTION
LEGAL STAFF
MEMBERSHIP
MAJOR PROGRAMS COMPLETED
MISC.

CAPSOC PARTY OF IOWA (IA)
DIRECTOR
ADDRESS
PHONE NO.
INCEPTION
LEGAL STAFF
MEMBERSHIP
MAJOR PROGRAMS COMPLETED
MISC.

CAPSOC PARTY OF KANSAS (KS)
DIRECTOR
ADDRESS
PHONE NO.
INCEPTION
LEGAL STAFF
MEMBERSHIP
MAJOR PROGRAMS COMPLETED
MISC.

CAPSOC PARTY OF KENTUCKY (KY0
DIRECTOR
ADDRESS
PHONE NO.
INCEPTION
LEGAL STAFF
MEMBERSHIP
MAJOR PROGRAMS COMPLETED
MISC.

CAPSOC PARTY OF LOUISIANA (LA)
DIRECTOR
ADDRESS
PHONE NO.
INCEPTION
LEGAL STAFF
MEMBERSHIP
MAJOR PROGRAMS COMPLETED
MISC.

CAPSOC PARTY OF MAINE (ME)
DIRECTOR
ADDRESS
PHONE NO.
INCEPTION
LEGAL STAFF
MEMBERSHIP
MAJOR PROGRAMS COMPLETED
MISC.

CAPSOC PARTY OF MARYLAND (MD)
DIRECTOR
ADDRESS
PHONE NO.
INCEPTION
LEGAL STAFF
MEMBERSHIP
MAJOR PROGRAMS COMPLETED
MISC.

CAPSOC PARTY OF MASSACHUSETTS (MA)
DIRECTOR
ADDRESS
PHONE NO.
INCEPTION
LEGAL STAFF
MEMBERSHIP
MAJOR PROGRAMS COMPLETED
MISC.

CAPSOC PARTY OF MICHIGAN (MI)
DIRECTOR
ADDRESS
PHONE NO.
INCEPTION
LEGAL STAFF
MEMBERSHIP
MAJOR PROGRAMS COMPLETED
MISC.

CAPSOC PARTY OF MINNESOTA (MN)
DIRECTOR
ADDRESS
PHONE NO.
INCEPTION
LEGAL STAFF
MEMBERSHIP
MAJOR PROGRAMS COMPLETED
MISC.

CAPSOC PARTY OF MISSISSIPPI (MS)
DIRECTOR
ADDRESS
PHONE NO.
INCEPTION
LEGAL STAFF
MEMBERSHIP
MAJOR PROGRAMS COMPLETED
MISC.

CAPSOC PARTY OF MISSOURI (MO)
DIRECTOR
ADDRESS
PHONE NO.
INCEPTION
LEGAL STAFF
MEMBERSHIP
MAJOR PROGRAMS COMPLETED
MISC.

CAPSOC PARTY OF MONTANA (MT)
DIRECTOR
ADDRESS
PHONE NO.
INCEPTION
LEGAL STAFF
MEMBERSHIP
MAJOR PROGRAMS COMPLETED
MISC.

CAPSOC PARTY OF NEBRASKA (NE)
DIRECTOR
ADDRESS
PHONE NO.
INCEPTION
LEGAL STAFF
MEMBERSHIP
MAJOR PROGRAMS COMPLETED
MISC.

CAPSOC PARTY OF NEVADA (NV)
DIRECTOR
ADDRESS
PHONE NO.
INCEPTION
LEGAL STAFF
MEMBERSHIP
MAJOR PROGRAMS COMPLETED
MISC.

CAPSOC PARTY OF NEW HAMPSHIRE (NH)
DIRECTOR
ADDRESS
PHONE NO.
INCEPTION
LEGAL STAFF
MEMBERSHIP
MAJOR PROGRAMS COMPLETED
MISC.

CAPSOC PARTY OF NEW JERSEY (NJ0
DIRECTOR
ADDRESS
PHONE NO.
INCEPTION
LEGAL STAFF
MEMBERSHIP
MAJOR PROGRAMS COMPLETED
MISC.

CAPSOC PARTY OF NEW MEXICO (NM)
DIRECTOR
ADDRESS
PHONE NO.
INCEPTION
LEGAL STAFF
MEMBERSHIP
MAJOR PROGRAMS COMPLETED
MISC.

CAPSOC PARTY OF NEW YORK (NY)
DIRECTOR
ADDRESS
PHONE NO.
INCEPTION
LEGAL STAFF
MEMBERSHIP
MAJOR PROGRAMS COMPLETED
MISC.

CAPSOC PARTY OF NORTH CAROLINA (NC)
DIRECTOR
ADDRESS
PHONE NO.
INCEPTION
LEGAL STAFF
MEMBERSHIP
MAJOR PROGRAMS COMPLETED
MISC.

CAPSOC PARTY OF NORTH DAKOTA (ND)
DIRECTOR
ADDRESS
PHONE NO.
INCEPTION
LEGAL STAFF
MEMBERSHIP
MAJOR PROGRAMS COMPLETED
MISC.

CAPSOC PARTY OF OHIO (OH)
DIRECTOR
ADDRESS
PHONE NO.
INCEPTION
LEGAL STAFF
MEMBERSHIP
MAJOR PROGRAMS COMPLETED
MISC.

CAPSOC PARTY OF OKLAHOMA (OK)
DIRECTOR
ADDRESS
PHONE NO.
INCEPTION
LEGAL STAFF
MEMBERSHIP
MAJOR PROGRAMS COMPLETED
MISC.

CAPSOC PARTY OF OREGON (OR)
DIRECTOR
ADDRESS
PHONE NO.
INCEPTION
LEGAL STAFF
MEMBERSHIP
MAJOR PROGRAMS COMPLETED
MISC.

CAPSOC PARTY OF PENNSYLVANIA (PA)
DIRECTOR
ADDRESS
PHONE NO.
INCEPTION
LEGAL STAFF
MEMBERSHIP
MAJOR PROGRAMS COMPLETED
MISC.

CAPSOC PARTY OF RHODE ISLAND (RI)
DIRECTOR
ADDRESS
PHONE NO.
INCEPTION
LEGAL STAFF
MEMBERSHIP
MAJOR PROGRAMS COMPLETED
MISC.

CAPSOC PARTY OF SOUTH CAROLINA (SC)
DIRECTOR
ADDRESS
PHONE NO.
INCEPTION
LEGAL STAFF
MEMBERSHIP
MAJOR PROGRAMS COMPLETED
MISC.

CAPSOC PARTY OF SOUTH DAKOTA (SD)
DIRECTOR
ADDRESS
PHONE NO.
INCEPTION
LEGAL STAFF
MEMBERSHIP
MAJOR PROGRAMS COMPLETED
MISC.

CAPSOC PARTY OF TENNESSEE (TN)
DIRECTOR
ADDRESS
PHONE NO.
INCEPTION
LEGAL STAFF
MEMBERSHIP
MAJOR PROGRAMS COMPLETED
MISC.

CAPSOC PARTY OF TEXAS (TX)
DIRECTOR
ADDRESS
PHONE NO.
INCEPTION
LEGAL STAFF
MEMBERSHIP
MAJOR PROGRAMS COMPLETED
MISC.

CAPSOC PARTY OF UTAH (UT)
DIRECTOR
ADDRESS
PHONE NO.
INCEPTION
LEGAL STAFF
MEMBERSHIP
MAJOR PROGRAMS COMPLETED
MISC.

CAPSOC PARTY OF VERMONT (VT)
DIRECTOR
ADDRESS
PHONE NO.
INCEPTION
LEGAL STAFF
MEMBERSHIP
MAJOR PROGRAMS COMPLETED
MISC.

CAPSOC PARTY OF VIRGINIA (VA)
DIRECTOR
ADDRESS
PHONE NO.
INCEPTION
LEGAL STAFF
MEMBERSHIP
MAJOR PROGRAMS COMPLETED
MISC.

CAPSOC PARTY OF WASHINGTON (WA)
DIRECTOR
ADDRESS
PHONE NO.
INCEPTION
LEGAL STAFF
MEMBERSHIP
MAJOR PROGRAMS COMPLETED
MISC.

CAPSOC PARTY OF WEST VIRGINIA (WV)
DIRECTOR
ADDRESS
PHONE NO.
INCEPTION
LEGAL STAFF
MEMBERSHIP
MAJOR PROGRAMS COMPLETED
MISC.

CAPSOC PARTY OF WISCONSIN (WI)
DIRECTOR
ADDRESS
PHONE NO.
INCEPTION
LEGAL STAFF
MEMBERSHIP
MAJOR PROGRAMS COMPLETED
MISC.

CAPSOC PARTY OF WYOMING (WY)
DIRECTOR
ADDRESS
PHONE NO.
INCEPTION
LEGAL STAFF
MEMBERSHIP
MAJOR PROGRAMS COMPLETED
MISC.

TERRITORIES

CAPSOC PARTY OF PUERTO RICO (PR)
DIRECTOR
ADDRESS
PHONE NO.
INCEPTION
LEGAL STAFF
MEMBERSHIP
MAJOR PROGRAMS COMPLETED
MISC.

CAPSOC PARTY OF SAMOA
DIRECTOR
ADDRESS
PHONE NO.
INCEPTION
LEGAL STAFF
MEMBERSHIP
MAJOR PROGRAMS COMPLETED
MISC.

CAPSOC PARTY OF GUAM
DIRECTOR
ADDRESS
PHONE NO.
INCEPTION
LEGAL STAFF
MEMBERSHIP
MAJOR PROGRAMS COMPLETED
MISC.

CAPSOC PARTY OF MARSHALL ISLANDS
DIRECTOR
ADDRESS
PHONE NO.
INCEPTION
LEGAL STAFF
MEMBERSHIP
MAJOR PROGRAMS COMPLETED
MISC.

[1] *The CapSoc Party is not to be confused with any other political party of similar doctrines. Our doctrines are as outlined in this book. CapSoc is the new but old socialist political party.

capsocpartyofamerica
POB #9407
chicago, IL 60609
United States
ph: 312/834/8074
Secretary: f.ottman77@yahoo.com

What We DO

Call Us Today

capsocpartyofamerica
POB #9407
chicago, IL 60609
United States
ph: 312/834/8074 Secretary: f.ottman77@yahoo.com

http://capsocpartyofamerica.com/